MADAM PANTALOONS:
GOLD RUSH PIONEER

by Jenifer E. Rowe

CONTENTS

CHAPTER 1
Early Years

J eanne Marie Suize (soo-WEEZ), who came to be known as Madam Pantaloons, was born in 1824 in the duchy of Savoie (sav-WAH), which later became part of France. Her village was located in the picturesque Thone Valley at the foot of the Alps. Although the area was lovely, during her growing years it was beset by crop failures, disease and poverty. She was the seventh of twelve children in the village of Thones, and their father owned an inn. The laws in France at that time stated that only the eldest son could inherit his parents' property, including the inn. All other sons and daughters needed to find their own livelihoods. So, Marie traveled to Paris at the age of 22 and tried to find work. After two years of struggle, she finally began a job at a newspaper, where she learned about the California gold rush.

Everyday life was difficult in France at that time. Women were sometimes unable to feed their children. People were unhappy about their hardships. Social unrest, including women's demands for the right to vote, led to a revolution that failed.

In 1848, Napoleon III claimed the title of President, and he soon went even further, naming himself Emperor. He began a campaign to convince the poor and unemployed citizens of France to emigrate to California in search of the newly discovered gold. Many French men and women with poor prospects for success at home followed his urgings and set sail for the American West. Marie decided to follow the direction that the emperor advised.

The French Revolution of 1848 arose partially from the widespread hunger and poor economic prospects of the population. Workers lost their jobs, bread prices rose, and people accused the government of corruption. The uprising was repressed by Napoleon III.

CHAPTER 2
Coming to California
❦

O n June 18, 1850, disguised as a male and accompanied by her younger brother Albert, Marie boarded a three-mast ship, the *Ferriere*. She declared herself to be a business traveler, and that was indeed her intention. The ship's route took them around Cape Horn at the southern tip of Chile, where the waters are particularly hazardous, owing to heavy winds, large waves, strong currents and icebergs. They reached the port of San Francisco five months later. Records do not explain why she cut her hair and wore masculine clothing for the entire trip, but it is easy to imagine that a young unmarried woman would be safer posing as a man on such a lengthy and dangerous sea journey.

After landing in San Francisco, Marie again dressed in the women's skirts and petticoats typical of the times, perhaps feeling protected by the company of brother Albert. The two of them did not stay long in San Francisco, however, where the muddy, crowded streets teemed with pioneers, traders, and adventurers. Their goal was to reach Jackson, where they had heard some of their fellow immigrants from Savoie had found opportunities in the gold mines. Jackson is just 37 miles south of

Sutter's Mill on the American River, where James Marshall discovered the first gold nugget on January 22, 1848.

4. JAMES MARSHALL, DISCOVERER OF GOLD, AT SUTTER'S MILL

James Marshall, an employee at Sutter's Mill in Coloma, California, discovered gold there in 1848. The news traveled quickly around the world and set off the California Gold Rush, which attracted more than 300,000 immigrants seeking their fortunes. Photo from Library of Congress.

CHAPTER 3
The Route to Jackson

In order to get from San Francisco to Jackson, Marie and Albert traveled by steamboat up the Sacramento River to the city of Sacramento. The riverboat was a new way to travel inland from the coast. In 1849, just one year after the beginning of the California Gold Rush, the first steamboat on the 382-mile-long Sacramento River began service between Sacramento and San Francisco. That first steamboat, the *George Washington*, soon had competition from over 300 other steamboats.

The California Gold Rush changed this river from a sleepy waterway to a bustling transportation highway. During the early years, the fare to Sacramento might have been $30, but as more river boats entered the market, the fare went down as low as one dollar. Competition among the steamboats led to many accidents.

Travel was harder after Marie and Albert reached the city of Sacramento. From there, they had to make their way on mules to the town of Jackson, in the heart of the gold country. After a long and difficult trip, the two found the mining camps at last, and with them, a good number of French miners.

The gold camps that they found in the hills around Jackson were filled with ragged, bearded men living in rough tents and shacks. When the miners saw Marie, they assumed she would be willing to make a living as their cook, laundress, dishwasher and mender of clothing. She declined their offers and insisted that she wanted to dig for gold alongside the men. Her proposal astonished them.

In one of these camps, Albert and Marie encountered people they knew, fellow immigrants from their home in Savoie. Marie recognized Andre Douet, and with a handshake agreement, Marie and Andre formed a business partnership in a mining concession. The agreement caused quite a stir among the other men, yet the partnership lasted 30 years.

Native Population

Before the arrival of men seeking their fortunes in gold, the area around present-day Jackson, California was occupied by Native Americans. For thousands of years, the Sierra Mi-Wuk called the place home. They inhabited areas along creeks, springs, flat ridges and terraces. The Mi-Wuks would forage and hunt in the area for seeds, acorns, grass and deer. The influx of gold miners and other settlers changed their surroundings and crowded them out.

Jackson

After 1848, gold seekers from around the world settled in and around Jackson, building a community with a diverse ethnic population, such as English, French, Chinese, Jews, and Italians. Many worked in the mines, some provided goods and services, and some became farmers and ranchers. It was often said that those who gained the most wealth from the gold rush were the vendors who sold shovels and groceries. A number of mines were opened up in Jackson. Over time, Jackson produced more than half the gold mined in the California gold rush.

CHAPTER 4
Mining Methods

The first miners to rush to the gold fields in California used pans to sift for gold in the riverbeds. Panning for gold was also known as "placer mining." Early miners sat by riverbeds, scooping wet soil into shallow metal pans. They swirled the pans, washing away the dirt and hoping to discover particles of gold.

Marie began her efforts at panning the day after finding the French camp. She was dressed in the long skirts and petticoats that she thought would be required of her to portray a serious businesswoman. Panning was hard work, standing all day knee-deep in icy water while sifting sand through a sieve to extract the gold. By the end of that first day, her clothes were torn and ruined, her shoes were filled with sand and mud, and the yards of wet cloth hanging from her waist prevented her from making any serious progress. The other miners laughed to see her struggles.

Marie went back to her tent at the end of the day and decided to make use of her brother's old trousers and boots. The next morning, with her hair again cut short and a hat pulled down over her head, she went back to her labors. More appropriately dressed, she was able to make much better progress in her work. She never put on a dress again.

Serious miners, including Marie, soon turned their efforts away from panning. Instead, using picks and shovels to dig deeper in the gravel, they hoped to extract more and larger gold nuggets. Eventually, sluice boxes were employed to sift through greater volumes of water. Wearing her trousers, or "pantaloons," Marie could dig harder and deeper for the gold. She spent many hours each day loosening the ground with a pickaxe and shoveling gravel into a sluice box to wash out the gold. She reportedly handled her tools as well as most of the men.

Women's Clothing

In the 1850s women's clothing had big ruffles and long skirts. In the daytime they wore jackets or bodices that buttoned down the front. The dress went over an undergarment so it could be visible under an open neck blouse or dress. The sleeves on the dresses were long, trimmed and designed with detail. Sometimes they wore collars and bows to tie the outfit together. In the evening or nighttime, they wore a crinoline (a steel cage) under their dresses to make them look bigger.

Mining Tools

Panning was known as "placer mining."

The sluices of the Gold Rush were usually long wood boxes with "riffles" in them to catch the gold. The intent was to get water to do most of the work of separating gold from dirt and gravel. The sluice boxes were placed in water at a slight downhill tilt so that water flowed through them, with enough current to wash out sand and gravel, but not enough to wash out the gold.

CHAPTER 5
Camp Life

T he work was hard, but Marie finally felt free, wearing the clothing that would allow her to work alongside the men in pursuing her dream of making her own living. Her fellow miners were shocked at first. In California – as in France – laws prevented women from wearing trousers. They could bare their legs in dance halls, but they were forbidden from covering their legs with pants. To be sure, other women had panned for gold - Indians and Mexicans and even American women. Some of the miners invited their wives and children to visit the camps and try their hands at panning for gold, but it was considered a fun adventure. None of those ladies wore pants. And no one was as successful as Marie Suize.

The living conditions in the camp were difficult. It was cold in the winter and hot in the summer. Food was scarce at times, with no fruits or vegetables to prevent diseases like scurvy. The mosquitoes and filth also brought malaria and cholera to plague them. Marie took some comfort that she and Albert were with many of their countrymen from Savoie. She tried to make life tolerable for the men, nursing them when they were ill and sometimes cooking a favorite dish that reminded them of their home across the ocean. The men eventually became her friends and protectors, giving her the nickname Marie *Pantalon* (French for *pants*.)

In every mining camp, the miners – mostly men- took turns cooking, a week at a time. Bread was a staple, and many men learned to bake bread as a part of their week's shift. Meat (including venison from deer hunting), potatoes and pickled vegetables rounded out the meals. Some of the men liked to cook, others hated it. Nevertheless, they all took their turns, and no one was excused from the duty. Poor cooks were teased for their lack of skills, but they were forgiven if the meal was at least edible. The cook was the first to rise in the morning, often serving a breakfast of warmed leftovers from the previous night's dinner, along with coffee and bread. The same cook often left the mining site early in order to start dinner preparations. One can imagine that Marie took her turn at cooking along with the rest of the crew, but she certainly would not have been singled out for being a woman. It is unlikely that she would have allowed it.

After dinner, the miners would gather to smoke their pipes around a campfire, telling stories and jokes to pass the time. We do not know whether Marie joined in their relaxation, although it seems doubtful that she would do so. She was a serious businesswoman with grander plans in mind, as she showed in the coming years.

A miner named Robert Butterfield wrote this account of camp life to his brother: "Thus we lived contentedly and happy. We worked as usual hard all day and sit around the fire-place with our boots off at night telling stories about what we heard and see, reading papers, re-reading old letters, reading books of whatever kind comes our way. Around the cheerful blaze too as we sit drying our feet at night we enjoy the wholesome pipe – occasionally indulging in a cigar."

CHAPTER 6
Team Leader

𝕸arie managed Andre's teams of workers in mining successful veins of gold. She signed the claim papers, led the teams, and defended the tunnels from claim jumpers as needed. The most famous of those skirmishes occurred in 1860, when a group of Canadian miners attempted to take over the tunnel on Humbug Hill that was claimed by Marie and Andre. The Canadians seized the tunnel and tried to force the French miners out. Marie's response was to set up camp at the opening of the tunnel, armed with two pistols and a soup bowl full of pepper. She and her team plugged up the ventilation hole and threatened to attack the Canadians with pepper if they didn't come out. The Canadians left, the air hole was reopened, and Marie's miners went back to work. Marie stayed at her post for eight days and nights. No one challenged any of her mines again, and some of the miners even referred to her as their Joan of Arc.

Building on her initial success, Marie eventually owned shares in mines and diggings throughout the gold country. Albert returned to France after a time. On her own visit back home, Marie tried to convince her sisters to join her in California, but none of them were interested. After that, Marie never returned to France. She had found a new life of freedom, and she would never give it up.

A great deal of work was involved in clearing a
tunnel mine. These tunnels were carefully
guarded and defended. Claim jumpers who
tried to gain control of others' stakes were
often met with armed resistance.

CHAPTER 7
Legal Troubles

In the 1860's, Marie and her business partner Andre Douet bought some land and began to grow grapes so that they could make wine. The French and the Italians were pioneers in producing the wine and brandy that Amador County is known for today. Marie was very successful with her vineyards, producing more wine than any other grower in the area.

The *Pacific Rural Press* reported on April 8, 1871, that "Mme. Marie Suize is the proprietress of a 800-acre tract of land … and is cultivating some 30,000 vines, and manufacturing about 12,000 gallons of wine… annually. With a view to silk raising, she is cultivating 3,000 mulberry trees." In this way, Marie put the soil on her ranch to work in order to expand her business.

Using the bounty of her vineyard, she opened wine shops in San Francisco and in Virginia City, Nevada. Since it was illegal at that time for women to appear in public wearing trousers, Marie had found it necessary to apply earlier for special permission from the lawmakers in Amador County to dress as she did. Opening businesses outside the county, however, exposed her to the laws in other locations. When she left Jackson and drove her wagon into Virginia City to check on her shop there, she was arrested for wearing pants. In the trial, she was simply told to put on a dress and to leave town.

A similar incident occurred in 1871, when Marie visited San Francisco on business and was again arrested for wearing pants.

As the *Gold Hill Daily News* reported on April 20, 1871, "Last evening a woman named Marie Suize was arrested in a saloon on Dupont Street on a charge of misdemeanor, by wearing the clothing commonly used by men…She is a woman about 29 or 30 years of age, and looks as though she was not afraid of work."

In her court appearance, she was fined five dollars by the judge and, as before, ordered to put on a dress. The newspapers of the time made quite a joke of her arrest, noting that it was said she looked better in men's clothing than she did in a dress. The *Daily Alta California* reported that some other female business owners had begun to express their interest in wearing trousers when it suited them as well.

The last time that Marie got into trouble for wearing pants was in Jackson itself, where a group of suffragettes took to the streets to support her cause. A jury was specially formed to settle the case. Marie stated that she had arrived on American soil wearing pants and had done so for the last eighteen years. The jurors decided that nothing terrible had occurred, and the men in the courtroom decided that the entire affair was a waste of time and that they would rather go hunting. Court was adjourned, and the men took off to hunt.

CHAPTER 8
A Proud Businesswoman
❦

Marie was proud of her nickname and even signed official documents with the name Marie Suize Pantalon. Over her lifetime, she became very wealthy from her gold mining and her wine production. Although she eventually lost almost all of that wealth gambling on investments in Nevada's Comstock Lode, she was always a businesswoman with a sense of adventure and possibility. Even after losing money in her investments, she still had the ranch that she shared with Andre, and that is where she spent the rest of her days. Marie Suize Pantalon lived her life the way she wanted to live it, free and unencumbered by the expectations of her gender. She died of pneumonia on January 8, 1892, and is buried somewhere in St. Patrick's Catholic Cemetery in Jackson, California, where a commemorative marker pays tribute to her memory.

MADAME PANTALON–THE NON-PAREIL

Marie Suize pantalon

The 1869 signature of Marie Suize aka Pantalon
on a petition that only men normally signed

IN MEMORY OF
'MADAME PANTALON'
JEANNE MARIE SUIZE,
BORN 14 JULY 1824
IN THÔNES, NOW IN FRANCE.
DIED 8 JANUARY 1892, NEAR CLINTON.
BURIED IN THIS CEMETERY IN
AN UNMARKED GRAVE.
EARLY PIONEER, GOLD MINE OWNER,
PROBABLY CALIFORNIA'S FIRST WOMAN
WINE AND BRANDY MAKER.

She preferred wearing a man's
pants rather than a woman's dress,
breaking custom. If not law in San
Francisco and Virginia City, In
Amador there is no evidence she
faced similar harassment
or indignity.

Plaque donated by The Quintors, 14 July 2004,
in cooperation with the Amador County Sesquicentennial Committee.

GLOSSARY:

Cholera: an acute infection caused by eating or drinking contaminated food or water.

Claim jumper: a person who seizes another's claim of land, especially for mineral rights.

Comstock Lode: the most valuable deposit of silver ore ever recorded, discovered in 1859 by Henry T. P. Comstock near Virginia City, Nevada.

Concession: a business arrangement or agreement.

Joan of Arc: a national heroine who at the age of seventeen took up arms to establish the rightful king on the French throne.

Malaria: a fever transmitted by mosquitoes.

Mulberry tree: a plant that is the exclusive food for the silkworm, which is reared for silk production.

Riffle: a shallow place in a river where water flows quickly past rocks. The model was used by gold miners in their sluice boxes to separate gold from gravel.

Scurvy: a disease caused by a lack of vitamin C, often provided by fruits and vegetables, and characterized by swollen bleeding gums.

Suffragette: a woman seeking the right to vote through organized protest.

BIBLIOGRAPHY

1. Butruille, Susan G. *Women's Voices from the Motherlode.* Boise, ID: Tamarack Books, Inc., 1998

2. Rohrbough, Malcolm J. *Days of Gold: The California Gold Rush and the American Nation.* University of California Press, 1997

3. Gold Hill Daily News. [volume], April 20, 1871

4. Daily Alta California, Volume 23, Number 7700, April 22, 1871

5. Daily Alta California, Volume 23, Number 7703, April 25, 1871

6. Pacific Rural Press, Volume 1, Number 14, April 8, 1871

Printed in the USA
CPSIA information can be obtained
at www.ICGtesting.com
LVHW052025131023
761043LV00012B/734